ENOUGH

poems by

Carolyn J. Fairweather Hughes

Finishing Line Press
Georgetown, Kentucky

ENOUGH

To my loving husband Richard,
who is the "tar baby" no more

ACKNOWLEDGMENTS

The following poems have previously appeared in the following literary magazines
and anthologies:

"Cohabitation" in *The Black Fly Review*
"A Kind of Loving", and "Stallions" in *The Vanderbilt Review*
"You're Always with Me" in *Calliopes Corner*
"Mirage", "Coupling" and "Afterthought" in *Kindred Spirit*
"On Target" in *Day Tonight/Night Today*
"Volcano in Mexico" in *Lucky Star*
"Closer Than Stars" and "The Nightmare" in *The Poet Peu a Peu*
"Vows" in *Yet Another Small Magazine*
"Late Summer Lies" in *Eve's Legacy*
"There Is a Dog That Barks" in *The Sow's Ear*
"Forgiveness" and "Tar Baby" in *Slant*
"After The Loving" in *The Bassettown Review*
"Testament" in *The Sacred Book*
"Rings" in *Forms*
"Deacon Jones and the Honkeytonk Hideaway" in *Lactucca*
"You Hurt My Head" in *Nycticorax*
"Symbiosis" in *Poets On*
"After the Loving" was published again in *The Great American Poetry Show, Volume 1*,
and in *Pittsburgh and Tri-State Area Poets*

Special thanks to my daughters Gabrielle and Rachel, and my granddaughters
Maya and Nora, and especially to my husband Richard, for all of their help and
encouragement.

Publisher: Leah Maines
Editor: Christen Kincaid
Cover Art: Gabrielle Jean Hughes
Author Photo: Richard W. Hughes
Cover Design: Elizabeth Maines McCleavy

Printed in the USA on acid-free paper.
Order online: www.finishinglinepress.com
            also available on amazon.com

Author inquiries and mail orders:
Finishing Line Press
P. O. Box 1626
Georgetown, Kentucky 40324
U. S. A.

Table of Contents

Cohabitation

I am the sheer white curtain
that blows across your face
on a summer morning

the lips of a girl
whose pale arms
hold you

the long lovely silences
when we both
float…

But deep in sleep
you turn from me
with a sigh

and caress
the aging body
of your wife.

Vows

You followed me that one dim night
through the bleak hours
of a convention drunk

I, in my silver fox and satin gown,
You, with an easy smile.

So comfortable together.

Softly, we touched
Felt the air   tremble
Blood quicken.

You led me away from
the thickening crowd.

But as the elevator
snapped shut,

I could not bring myself
to break
the sanctity

of that one golden moment,
when I first lifted the veil
to another.

Volcano in Mexico

Shivering in my summer cotton
I stop to tie straps on sandaled feet
cut and bleeding from the climb.

You do not wait
but disappear into clouds
as you make for the rim.

Lightheaded from thin air
you are obsessed
with reaching the edge
of this dead rock.

Below, clouds close in
suspending me in a cold,
unearthly calm.

I hunker down
rub my arms warm
and call to you softly.

But, as ghostly fingers of mist
seize me, a great chill
wracks my body.

I feel my throat tighten
feet freeze in step.

I try to climb
but am unable to go
either up or down.

I twist the thin circle of gold
around and around on my finger.

Teeth chatter violently
lips fight to speak

I spit out your name,
My voice a scream   strange
wooden   an entity apart
from me.

Magically, you materialize
eyes hard set
staring straight ahead
mouth taut.

You grab my hand
and pull me
back down to the village
and the smell of burning
rosewood.

There Is a Dog That Barks

There is a dog that barks
just enough to wake me up
then stops…

so that I think I dreamt
his bark.

The even breathing of the husband beside me
breaks uneasily
upon my splintered sleep.

I see a girl in her narrow virgin bed
staring out at the full clean moon,
the tall straight pine.

Her simple clarity
sends chills up my spine.

I reach out to brush her cheek
but touch only cracks
bleeding light.

And there is this dog that barks,
just enough to wake me up
then stops...

Night Moves

The intense arc of your arm
cracks me so close
I cannot sleep.

The need to escape
your embrace
possesses me.

While hard fingers
of a roughened palm trace
my warm path through sheets.

The Nightmare

Love lies between them
like a frightened child
who has climbed into their bed
for comfort.

Her nightmare was too real
for sleep. She cannot close
her eyes for fear it will
catch her unaware.

They take turns reassuring her
it was only a bad dream
but not before each of them remembers
what it was like to wake up

alone and afraid
in the middle of the night.

Self-Defense

I do not sharpen
hard points of hatred
to draw your blood.

But to defend myself
against the warm underbelly
of your love

Whose white-eyed flint
strikes my skin
with unchecked lust:

A flaming tongue that
Turns the me I know
into a charred stump

of self.

On Target

He is shooting in the cellar;
I can smell powder burning;
and the sharp snap of the report
breaks in upon my thoughts
like the brisk crack of a whip
meeting flesh.

I see the bullets miss
last year's telephone book

Seek a fault in the cement block wall
and send the whole house crashing
down into the old coal mine shaft
that sits and waits for such
recklessness.

But when he comes up
wearing that cool smile,

I fight the urge to
grab the gun,
calmly turn the page
of some pre-possessing book
and try, very hard,
not to look.

Wild Turkey

We were making love in late October,
when we first saw them down below—
a flock of black feathers
camouflaged by curled leaves.

They were still in season,
well within range of his rifle sights.
But, it was taboo
to hunt on Sunday.

I imagined him returning—
the rifle aimed
his finger on the trigger
as if it were a tit,

the sharp crack
like a slap
feathers flying
the flock in frenzy.

"That's the first I've seen so many,"
he said, smiling,
as he marked our spot—
a bed of dried leaves on top of the ridge.

As we walked away from the wild turkeys
through poison ivy, bike trails,
and stickerbushes,
I thought of Thanksgiving:

him plucked and stuffed.

You Hurt My Head

You hurt my head
with your cacophony.
I hold palms over ears
to stop the brittle shock
of words,

but I cannot take my eyes
from your mouth,
the way it moves
animating
a silent screen face.

I smile
mime your pouting lips
and dream your voice
a ribbon of blue silk
that gently strokes my skin.

Rings

The man who is losing his wife
Works wood with his hands
He sings as he works
His fingers fondly feeling the grain—
A former pulse of life locked in rings.
For as long as the instrument he is making sounds
The spirit of the tree will live.

After his wife has gone
He plucks the dulcimer and sings
The strings play, the wood resonates the sound
Made richer, deeper by the tree's life
Locked within its rings.
For as long as the dulcimer he is playing lives
The spirit of his love will sing.

Closer Than Stars

Some dawns, I waltz back barefoot
through mauve-colored morning
to keep the clack of my heels
from cracking your dreams.

Softly, I slip out
of shimmering silk
and bury myself
in your warmth.

I stretch to kiss
your sleeping face.

You half-awake
and press
the cool shape
of my body
closer than stars.

Conditioning

Your pale fingers rim
the glass of Chablis
like glowing filaments.

sparks strike my skin
Burn nerve endings
to bone.

The pain shrieks
in a single ache
to my brain,

where it stirs
alternate layers
of wetness and waiting.

They calm my impulse
to seize your fingertips
in my lips.

Instead
I sit
silently   and wait

for the gentle touch
of your hand
on mine.

Sucked Down Screaming

We climb aboard The Thunderbolt
the biggest wooden rollercoaster
in the world.

You pull back the safety bar
and put your arm around me.
I am a little afraid,
but I want the fun.

As the car creaks upward,
your ribbon-like thrill
silkens my throat.

I swallow your smile
and hold onto the taste
of your tongue.

My palms sweat,
as we inch closer
and closer to the top.

I grip the slippery bar
as tight as I can.

You hold me tighter.

At the top,
the car seems to hover.
The world below
slows to a stop.

For a moment, time
stands still.

We both take a deep breath,
and hold onto
each other

until,
gravity
sucks us down

screaming...

The Kingdom of Need

Afterwards, you sit
completely clothed
on an edge of the motel bed,
and watch me
apply kohl to eyes
that glow
like deep-water,
phosphorescent fish.

We are accustomed to the subtle
language of darkness
and understand the risks
of swimming at such depth.
But, there is nothing here,
in this room,
that we have not been through
before.

I watch you watching me,
as I stroke blush on cheeks
and line lips with Silver City Pink.
You smile softly
in that rare, relaxed way
that only I know,
point to my lids and say:
"You forgot the blue."

The furrow in your brow fades
and I see the man I met so long ago,
when your eyes leapt out at me
and you laughed easily.
It is a kind of peace we have come to,
a resigned half-having,
like a kingdom we can come to
when we need.

A Kind of Loving

The parts of my body
that stir
the rough edges of eyes
ache for the quick, heated touching.

I hold your last hug
so close
that my arms break
on its bulk.

The lullaby lingers
in my loins
like the quick-clicking heels
of the olive-eyed dancer.

How can I love you so little
and want you so much?

Perhaps our bodies know us better.

And before we leave
the little room so far out
to step into those other selves,

Kiss me once more

so our false lips
can serenade
the sting.

Commitment

You stare from the safety
of a barren cage.

There are tears in your eyes.

My full lips
brush against the bars.

You inch back
believing in a bond
stronger than love.

Faces flush
as your body pulses
with the taut force
of its need for me.

My nipples harden,
but you draw back
clutch the narrow bed,
         the rusty sink

And say softly,
"Forever?"

I hold out my hand
nod slowly
and the bars
             melt.

Deacon Jones and the Honkytonk Hideaway

Painted red, white, and blue,
it stuck out
like a flag.

"Rural tacky!"
his wife would've
sneered

at the starglow ceiling,
the sharp disinfectant smell.

But the girl wove walls
into wood, sheets
into cool, feathery ferns.

Her soft moss skin
touched his boyhood,
and Deacon Jones lay

smiling
in fields full
of young birches

his face forever buried
in rich
purple clover.

Mirage

I bathe
in undulating waves
of a smile
that stirs embers
of a faded fire.

Black holes of eyes
still suck in my senses
Make me smoulder in hot sand
Thirst for your mouth.

But other lips wash away
the taste of grit
the emptiness
of ash.

Coupling

They splice in frenzy
short circuiting
other connections
for an electric flash

that plunges them
into a blinding pitch
from which only the slight
crackling of filament sounds

as it arcs gracefully
outward into the pinwheeled
paradox of space.

After the Loving

Naked,
I stand shivering
as daybreak guillotines dreams.

You shrug,
and shower off
my smell.

I smooth out a silken blouse
and straighten the collar
on your pin-striped shirt.

You kiss me matter-of-factly
as if you're just going to the corner
for a quart of milk,
then head for the door,
whistling.

I try not to look,
but relent at the last minute,
just in time
to catch the ache
in your eyes.

Stallions

At first it is fun.
I, with a foot on the backs
of the roan and the black,
urge them on with the reins
and a slight pinch of bit.

Galloping side by side,
they usurp my gentle hand.
Fierce animal eyes flash.
Mouths froth with the fever of flight.

The roan races toward
the wild reaches of the woods
strewn with violets and crabapples.

But the black charges
for the top of the sand dunes
where the ocean looms blue and brilliant.

My bare toes dig into their skin.
Hands grip the slippery reins.

They no longer listen.

I know I must choose:
either to let go of one
or be thrown
under thudding hooves.

I choose to hold on
until I   am thrown
or they   run out of breath.

It is   enough.

Afterthought

The gentle sadness
in your eyes
penetrates bone.

To soothe the ache
my full lips apply
hot, compressed kisses.

Words cannot wash away
the wound
or hide the scar.

All I can do,
Perhaps,
is stop the blood

Tar Baby

Silence gathers
around you
like tar
thick, opaque
impermeable.

I try to shape it
into the words
I want to hear,
into the flat
surface of a road
with long white lines,
fluorescent signs.

But you,
you say
nothing.

My fingers
like my words
stick in your silence—
huge wireless
telephone poles.

I draw back
try to work
my way free,
but every move
sucks me deeper
into your
sullen darkness.

But you,
you say
nothing.

As thick layers
of silence
begin to cover me,

I think I hear
the muffled sound
of a voice fighting
to clear itself.

Then, I realize
it is only
my own heart
beating blood
back into a brain
full of tar.

And you,
you, of course,
say
nothing.

Hard Time

O love,
you oblique sorcerer,
whose tricks I catch
with one eye,
and that peripherally,

you sentence me
to twenty years'
hard labor
pounding a monolith
that resists, resists.

I fail to find
the crack that splits
this smiling stone.

Then,
when I least suspect,
he opens up
dazzling me
with an innocence

fresh
as our baby's
first breath.

Adversary

In the public heat and sweat
of an asphalt court
we bat yellow tennis balls
back and forth.

I keep whacking them
high and clear
over the chainlink fence
into waist high weeds.

You watch   wondering
if I'm doing it deliberately
to make you miss your chance
at volleying them back.

But you mellow when you see
my full mouth-open laugh
as I watch them sail
out of your swing.

What you fail to see
what I will never let you see
in that smile are the poised
sharpened points of my teeth.

Late Summer Lies

I will chase my shadowed dream
on an orange slice of moon
through slight, stirring wind,

while you bend
tall golden grass
for a rustle
of red taffeta.

An August storm
may crack the wooded limb
and leave an endless strew
of broken twigs, bowed evergreens.

But this freak flash
cannot snap
my thorny stalk
or uproot our rose.

And we shall lie together
in late summer grass
our nostrils filled with the fragrance

of scattered
rose
petals.

Forgiveness

I splinter at your sincerity,
want to break its bleat
with a snide look, a sarcasm, perhaps,
but cannot bring myself to it.

The words I have heard before,
but there is something about the tone that aches
like the loss of a first love.

And that damned familiar innocence
sings
in the silence
between us—

High, clear notes,
fresh
as the face
of a ten year -old choir boy.

Point of View

If we could scrub out the scuffs,
specks of coal dust,
brown stain of blood on sheets,
and come to each other fresh
as unscythed hay
or a stream without metal,
Could we love each other better?

Our feet tremble on this fragile planet
that from the moon glows blue,
and bodies flow with the spinning
of its days and nights,
yet, in sleep we clasp each other close
and dream   our love brighter
than stars.

Testament

We come together
softly
in half-light

bodies thicker
whiter
more fragile

than we remember

The unspoken
tenderness
Testament

to something
stubborn
that survives

like honeysuckle
on barbed wire

You're Always with Me

You're always with me
             even when you're not
Through you I…

see goodness in the way
moss covers rough bark
with soft green;

hear music in the low voice
of a mourning dove
cooing to its mate;

tingle at the fresh smell
of black soil; and

savor the sweet
succulence of peach.

The texture of your touch
lingers on my fingertips

imprinting me
with the nubile softness
of lips.

You infuse all parts of me
with the sublime loveliness
that is our most intimate union

Enough

It is not enough for me to love you
in the half-light of fern forests,
when the scent of lilac and fresh black soil
is everywhere, and you also are lilac, fresh
and everywhere.

It is not enough for you to love me
when honeysuckle sweetens breath
and breath itself is but a pause
in sweet, sweet panting.

But you must love me
in those thorny, ragged days,
when I irritate easily
and speak to you sharper
than I should.

And, I must love you
when you push me away
and curl up inside
like a moth regressing.

And we must love each other
through all the treaded minutes
in-between tender,

until suddenly, I smile,
or suddenly, you smile,

bring out the brandy snifters
and sit inhaling
the dark, amber liquid,

lips barely touching the rim
as the taste thickens
on tongues.

And in that one golden moment,
we understand
what enough is.

Symbiosis

I don't know anymore
where you end and I begin,
When I look into your eyes
I see myself
as you must see me.

You know each curve and cleft
better than I.
To me   my body is a mystery.

But I know the history
of each hair on your chest,
the chasm of your navel,
the insides of ears
as familiar as thirst.

I touch you not as other
but as part of
myself.

Each night
we fall asleep
in each other's arms
and wake up
holding ourselves.

A native of Englewood Cliffs, New Jersey, **Carolyn Jean Fairweather Hughes** lived with her maternal grandparents for three years during World War II when her father was fighting on an aircraft carrier in the Pacific Ocean. She is the oldest of seven children. Carolyn now lives in Pittsburgh, PA. with Richard, her husband of 53 years. He is a retired trainman and traditional musician and singer. They have two daughters, Gabrielle Jean Hughes and Rachel Anne Hughes-Doichev, and two granddaughters, Maya Doichev and Nora Doichev. The entire family live close to each other and visit frequently.

Carolyn graduated from Duquesne University and worked as a reporter and editor for newspapers in New Jersey and Pittsburgh. She also served as a communications specialist for the Pittsburgh Board of Public Education and retired from the Allegheny County Court of Common Pleas. Her poetry has appeared in many literary magazines including *Wind, Pleiades, Slant, SageWoman, The Vanderbilt Review, The Pittsburgh Quarterly,* and others. Her poems have appeared in such anthologies as *We Speak for Peace, For She Is the Tree of Life, Pittsburgh and Tri-State Area Poets, Cathedral Poets, The Great American Poetry Show, Vol. I, Pennsylvania Seasons,* and the popular *When I Am an Old Woman, I Shall Wear Purple.*

Carolyn and Richard enjoy hiking, biking, traveling out west and abroad, reading, classical and traditional music, theater, films, and spending time with their family.